Plant Parts
Seeds

Revised Edition

by Vijaya Khisty Bodach

Consulting Editor: Gail Saunders-Smith, PhD

Consultant: Judson R. Scott, Former President
American Society of Consulting Arborists

CAPSTONE PRESS
a capstone imprint

Pebble Plus is published by Capstone Press,
1710 Roe Crest Drive, North Mankato, Minnesota 56003.
www.mycapstone.com

Copyright © 2007, 2016 by Capstone Press, a Capstone imprint. All rights reserved.

No part of this publication may be reproduced in whole or in part, or stored in a retrieval system, or transmitted in any form or by any means, electronic, mechanical, photocopying, recording, or otherwise, without written permission of the publisher. For information regarding permission, write to Capstone Press, 1710 Roe Crest Drive, North Mankato, Minnesota 56003.

Library of Congress Cataloging-in-Publication Data is available on the Library of Congress website.

ISBN: 978-1-5157-4246-3 (revised paperback)
ISBN: 978-1-5157-4355-2 (ebook pdf)

Editorial Credits
Sarah L. Schuette, editor; Jennifer Bergstrom, designer; Kelly Garvin, photo researcher/photo editor

Photo Credits
Capstone Studio: Karon Dubke, Cover, 1; Shutterstock: Bogdan Wankowicz, 7, bottom 22, Colin Edwards Wildside, 11, iwka, 17, Kathy Clark, 21, Laura Bartlett, middle 22, lovelyday12, 15, Steve McWilliam, 9, takegraph, right 22, tcareob72, 19, Thomas Mounsey, 5, VLADIMIR DUDKIN, 13

Note to Parents and Teachers

The Plant Parts set supports national science standards related to identifying plant parts and the diversity and interdependence of life. This book describes and illustrates seeds. The images support early readers in understanding the text. The repetition of words and phrases helps early readers learn new words. This book also introduces early readers to subject-specific vocabulary words, which are defined in the Glossary section. Early readers may need assistance to read some words and to use the Table of Contents, Glossary, Read More, Internet Sites, and Index sections of the book.

Table of Contents

Plants Need Seeds............ 4
Spreading Seeds 10
Seeds We Eat 16
Wonderful Seeds 20

Parts of a Pea Plant 22
Glossary 23
Read More 23
Index 24
Internet Sites.............. 24

Plants Need Seeds

Plants make seeds.
Each seed can grow
into a new plant.

5

Seeds need **soil**, water,

and warmth to grow.

Seeds break open in soil.

Stems grow up.

Roots grow down.

7

The new plant makes leaves, flowers, and fruit.

Seeds grow inside the fruit.

Spreading Seeds

Birds help spread seeds when they eat berries. The seeds come out in their **waste** and fall to the ground.

Weather spreads seeds.
Dandelion seeds float
to new places with the wind.

People scatter seeds.
Pumpkin seeds grow well
in large gardens.

Seeds We Eat

Many seeds are good to eat.

Peas are soft seeds

that grow in pods.

Sunflower seeds
make crunchy snacks.
These hard seeds grow
in the middle of sunflowers.

Wonderful Seeds

Large or small, hard or soft, seeds grow into new plants.

Parts of a Pea Plant

stem

seed

roots

flower

leaves

pod

Glossary

root—the parts of a plant that grow mostly underground; roots take in water and food from the soil.

soil—the dirt where plants grow; most plants get their food and water from the soil.

stem—the long main parts of a plant that makes leaves; food gathered by roots moves through stems to the rest of the plant.

waste—the part of food that isn't used by the body; people and animals get rid of waste.

Read More

Branigan, Carrie, and Richard Dunne. *Flowers and Seeds.* World of Plants. North Mankato, Minn.: Smart Apple Media, 2005.

Farndon, John. *Seeds.* World of Plants. San Diego: Blackbirch Press, 2005.

Mattern, Joanne. *How Peas Grow.* How Plants Grow. Milwaukee: Weekly Reader, 2006.

Index

berries, 10

birds, 10

fruit, 8

leaves, 8

peas, 16

people, 14

pumpkin seeds, 14

roots, 6

soil, 6

stems, 6

sunflowers, 18

weather, 12

Word Count: 124
Grade: 1
Early-Intervention Level: 14

Internet Sites

FactHound offers a safe, fun way to find Internet sites related to this book. All of the sites on FactHound have been researched by our staff.

Here's how:

1. Visit www.facthound.com

2. Choose your grade level.

3. Type in this book ID 073686346X for age-appropriate sites. You may also browse subjects by clicking on letters, or by clicking on pictures and words.

4. Click on the Fetch It button.

Facthound will fetch the best sites for you!